As

Love

MW01110211

The Collected Works on Asatru

Includes: Love and Hate in Asatru, Inguz; Developing
The God Seed, Raidho; The Long Journey of Life;
Living In The Shadow of Baldur's Death

Ansuz; Business, Life and The Valfathers
Example

The Soldiers Edda

Voluspa and Havamal Pocket Sized for the
Troops

Understanding Asatru

Asatru Awakening

Nobility

Hail to the giver! / a guest has come

Where shall the stranger sit?

~ 3 ~

Aegir's Feast

Bryan Wilton

ISBN-10: 1541213645

ISBN-13: 978-1541213647

~ 5 ~

Contents

Preface...7

Chapter One 10

Chapter Two 35

Chapter Three 78

Chapter Four...86

Preface

     I think we might all be able to agree that
the lore we typically refer to in Asatru has more
than one meaning. I have, on countless
occasions, spent long hours speaking with and
helping people through the various difficulties
associated with their lives. In some instances, it
seems to click almost immediately. While in
other cases I will have expounded upon some
fantastic point of understanding which to my
mind would help the individual alleviate the
problems they are encountering, only to have it
repeated back to me in an almost unintelligible
manner. Nothing of what I had said made any

sense to them and usually there are deep seated neurosis which preclude the individual from accepting the proposals put forth.

But the success of my suggestions in any given scenario is not the point of this book. The creation of a suitable environment within the mind for the continual remediation of said difficulties is. We are fortunate enough to have a fantastic example of just how to do this within the lore which we possess.

The Lay of Hymir, Loki's Wrangling and the description of Hel's realm contain a rich and wonderful tapestry which, when studied with a nautical standard towards a healthy mental and emotional state, provides us with a fantastic backdrop to guide the actions of our thinking processes.

The cultivation of an august thought process with regards to the future we wish to develop for ourselves is far more than just wishful thinking. It is an achievable state of mind one might considering to be a fine blessing of living an Asatru life. All along it has been right there in front of us.

Just like our learned thought patterns, the focus of these tales has been upon the negative.

It was the easiest thing for me to view at first as well. Now let's look at it again; with an emphasis on much more than just the suggestion of what not to do. We are going to take it somewhat past the simple avoidance of insulting the gods or getting in their way. We are going to use it to form a manner by which we may emulate these same actions with regards to our thinking and our actions. We will use it to enable us to make sound and timely decisions with regards to just who we are going to allow into our lives. We are going to watch our lives take a turn for the better in the most unexpected of ways. We are going to see exactly how to achieve our goals.

Thank you for joining me on this journey as you have with so many of my other works. Each one has been a learning and sometimes very cathartic process. Each literary endeavor has been, to many people around the world, a feast for a very hungry folk soul. So let us again feast upon the wisdom of a long past age. I hope it provides as much an impetus for the creation of something great in your life as it has in mine.

Bryan D. Wilton 15 Dec 2016

Chapter One

In almost all the great literature we have which pertains to the spiritual aspect of history; feasting is an important tradition. But I think almost anyone who would read this book might agree that the description of the feast is more than just a literary attempt to set the stage. From Beowulf to King Arthur and the Knights of the Round Table, to the Last Supper and the Marriage feast of Canna, to the feasting table we are preparing to discuss in depth; Aegir's Feast; there is a wealth of information and suggestions as to how we might "set the table" as it were with regards to how we feast upon the abundance of life.

The romanticized literature of the middle ages and the composition of several cultures which resulted in the big three monotheistic faiths offer us similar suggestions about this feasting tradition. In just about every case there are a few consistent themes. That the assembled individuals are each unique in their personas, that the meal is a grand one with the suggestion of miraculous occurrences and that everyone will walk away from the table on their way to whatever destiny awaits them. Full of the "meal" they require to handle the arduous tasks before them and achieve what greatness may lie in wait.

These fantastic tales have been told for centuries in one form or another but it is in the lore of the Northern Europeans, specifically the Poetic and Prose Eddas which put forth a tale full of meanings we need only to decipher to set a table for the heroic undertakings of our own life.

The Lay of Hymir outlines the preparation necessary to set such a feast. It talks of the ordeals we need to overcome, the state mind which prompts such an undertaking and the location along with the necessary implements. Let's take a look at this age old story and see if we might surmise as to why it has existed for as long as it has.

It begins as thus:

1. *Of old the gods* | *made feast together,*

And drink they sought | *ere sated they were;*

Twigs they shook, | *and blood they tried:*

Rich fare in Ægir's | *hall they found.*

It is of no small significance that the gods have found the rich fare they have in the realm of the ocean giant. I'm not talking about fish either. It appears that the gods have what amounts to be an insatiable appetite. But I think it is more along the lines of a strong and continuous desire to get our attention.

The twigs they shook might be the world tree; Yggdrasil and its creation or the rune staves so hard earned from the all-father. We are all well aware that it is our actions which provide the fresh water which the Norns use to nourish, not only the roots of the tree of our life but that of Yggdrasil as well. Mighty sticks indeed.

The blood is from the Blots we hold to sway the gods opinion in our favor, to give thanks and exchange a gift for a gift. But it would appear that there is something falling short in the relationship between men and gods. Or perhaps there is something which men ought to know but do not. The hunger with which the divine desires to associate with men is never sated. But it is not something we are just given. If the initiate were to be handed the wisdom, power and understanding as represented by our pantheon of Gods and Goddesses, we would find ourselves overwhelmed in short order given the current understanding of faith within the Asatru community. We must earn our seat at the table. That means we are going to have to develop along the spiritual lines intended for us. As with most significant events in the lore with regards to Odin; he will ensure the odds are in his favor. If we look carefully we will see the path we are supposed to take. I cannot imagine Odin's interest in us would be anything less than the attention he has paid to so many other details.

So they decide that it is within the rich realm of the ocean where they will find their greatest fulfillment. And for good reason. Water is a powerful symbol across time, geography and culture as something which is holy. It represents life in almost every corner of the globe. Its sacred aspects are evidenced in the runes as Laguz, Issa, and Hagalaz. Each one a representation of water in various states of existence and possibility. The fact that the majority of our being and everything else on earth which walks, talks, crawls or grows is comprised of water is also important to note. It is a connecting element of our physical forms. But it is also a representation of our minds. Not the brain, but the powerful spiritual aspect of our being science is just now beginning to understand and which religion has long taken advantage of.

And just like the water which is vital to life, our minds will assume the shape of the container we place them in. It is very important that the readers of this book understand that the choice of container we wish to use is our idea and no one else's. Much of what I have written suggests that this container is formed when we are very young by the ideals and attitudes of our parents, churches, schools and geographic location. Suffice it to say that the vessel we may have been given is not suitable for the greatness the gods wish of us. Nor is it suitable for the greatness which we are built for.

Just as Rig once walked the earth imparting the divine blessing which he did, Odin brings the full force of assembled Asgard to feast within the containers which represent our minds. For it is our minds which create the reality we live in. The moment Odin notices what is going on it is written down as such:

> 2. *The mountain-dweller | sat merry as boyhood,*
>
> *But soon like a blinded | man he seemed;*
>
> *The son of Ygg | gazed in his eyes:*
>
> *"For the gods a feast | shalt thou forthwith get."*

For much of our life we are content to indulge in the passions and moods so prominent in a society dominated by the extremes of youth.

But that joyous playground of the immature mind will not bring about the results expected when Odin, Vili and Ve offered us good sense and a host of other gifts. The giants have always been the primal and immature forces of nature and life. Base and instinctive, ruled by passions and shortcomings. To see one indulging in prosperity within the realm of the emotion driven humankind must assuredly be offensive to the high minded ideals of sky gods. So a challenge is set. A goal if you will. To set a feast for the gods. It is a goal each one of us must also undertake. To set, within our minds, a feast whereby the blessing of the divine might fully be brought to bear on our existence in a manner congruent with our creation. That is; to develop into something far greater than was imagined when we were given the containers to hold our dreams in when we were young. Notice that it is the warder of mankind who sets the challenge. To join him in a heroic undertaking.

The roiling tides of life are an ever-present aspect of living in the forms which we now inhabit. Ups and downs, successes and failures are largely determined by who we allow to sit at our feast. Or more importantly which aspects of the divine as represented by our thoughts and emotions do we allow to fill the containers which represent the mind of our being. Will you attempt to cram the truly fantastic proportions of your allotment into a beer bottle or would you rather that the mead of inspiration be brewed with a cauldron of cosmic proportions? It would seem that Odin wishes our inspiration to emanate from a truly endless supply. One which might sate the gods and fulfill the grandest of our dreams. To whit:

> 3. *The word-wielder toil | for the giant worked,*
>
> *And so revenge | on the gods he sought;*
>
> *He bade Sif's mate | the kettle bring:*
>
> *"Therein for ye all | much ale shall I brew."*

At first glance it would appear to be a resentment at the mind controlling our passions. No one likes to deny the heart that which it wants. And the powerful being which rules the oceans most certainly represents our emotional state in this tale. But the Gods have not chosen the realm of the ocean to enslave and conquer it, they have assembled to enjoy the bounty of it. It is curious since apparently Asgard has more than enough. The successful endeavor will yield a fine union of the heart and the mind to create more than we might ever imagine. It is a very powerful example of creating a balance in our lives which will yield results we cannot fathom when we are firmly in the grips of an all mental or emotional state of being.

All too often people will drift from one extreme of the other. The all mental being lacks personality and spirit, while the passionate individual lacks the mental fortitude to withstand the storm. The union of the Aesir and the Vanir is our first hint that the heart and the mind must act as one to feast in the gleaming halls of the Asgard we might build for ourselves. It is also just a first step.

> 4. *The far-famed ones | could find it not,*
>
> *And the holy gods | could get it nowhere;*
>
> *Till in truthful wise | did Tyr speak forth,*
>
> *And helpful counsel | to Hlorrithi gave.*

It is the age old wisdom of our grandfathers and grandmothers whose hearts and minds have been tempered with age which will provide us with the wisdom and truth which originates in the union of the heart and mind. Tyr is the finest example of such a character as may be espoused. The suggestions that he may have been the original sky god before Odin places him in that respected position of an elder in my eyes. His understanding of the sacrifice he must make for the good of the tribe is nowhere better detailed than when he loses a hand to the Fenris wolf. How could he have not known when they were planning the rope to bind the wolf that someone would have to accept the responsibility of the deceit. But knowing with his mind and acting with his heart, his tribe will enjoy a period of peace where the people he loves might enjoy life. And again he comes forward with wisdom so that others of us who have ears to hear and eyes to see might revel in that peace as well. Just like our grandparents who would wish to see us succeed at anything we do and often times they will take measures necessary to ensure it can be; Tyr comes forward and demonstrates his knowledge and a willingness to face the fear of his origins.

5. *"There dwells to the east | of Elivagar*

Hymir the wise | at the end of heaven;

A kettle my father | fierce doth own,

A mighty vessel | a mile in depth."

Thor spake:

6. *"May we win, dost thou think, | this whirler of water?"*

Tyr spake:

"Aye, friend, we can, | if cunning we are."

Courage, Strength and Wisdom set forth to face the great unknown and secure for the future generation and the seated assembly a vessel so vast that there is no limit to the dreams and successes it might bring forth. It is the same thing with us. We must use courage, strength and wisdom to face those limitations we have been given. We should set about to clearing away the conditioning we have been given in order to fully accept those divine gifts we have been holding on too for so long. Holding on too, fully aware of and completely unable to put them to use in our life. The union of our heart and mind when focused upon a goal gives us an almost unlimited access to the divine. These gods and goddesses represent our own inner powers and faculties which enable us to realize our own desires. It is our responsibility to create an inviting place within our minds where these aspects of ourselves might thrive. Some of us will need it when the scope of the limitations we must remove becomes evident.

7. Forward that day | with speed they fared,

From Asgarth came they | to Egil's home;

The goats with horns | bedecked he guarded;

~ 20 ~

Then they sped to the hall | where Hymir dwelt.

8. The youth found his grandam, | that greatly he
loathed,

And full nine hundred | heads she had;

But the other fair | with gold came forth,

And the bright-browed one | brought beer to her
son.

Notice that it is a feminine figure which
offers the cup. This is a repeated theme in the
feasting tradition of the North.

9. "Kinsman of giants, | beneath the kettle

Will I set ye both, | ye heroes bold;

For many a time | my dear-loved mate

To guests is wrathful | and grim of mind."

A second important aspect of the feminine
in the feasting tradition is where the stranger
may sit. In this case it is her son. Who has gone
on the greater things, with a very powerful tribe.
He has left the simple beginning behind and
returns with honor to lay claim to a remnant of
his heritage which he is now worthy to own.

10. Late to his home | the misshapen Hymir,

The giant harsh, | from his hunting came;

The icicles rattled | as in he came,

For the fellow's chin-forest | frozen was.

11. "Hail to thee, Hymir! | good thoughts mayst
thou have;

Here has thy son | to thine hall now come;

(For him have we waited, | his way was long;)

And with him fares | the foeman of Hroth,

The friend of mankind, | and Veur they call him.

A heroes introduction and a
reminder that he has achieved what he set out to
accomplish.

12. "See where under | the gable they sit!

Behind the beam | do they hide themselves."

The beam at the glance | of the giant broke,

And the mighty pillar | in pieces fell.

13. Eight fell from the ledge, | and one alone,

The hard-hammered kettle, | of all was whole;

Forth came they then, | and his foes he sought,

The giant old, | and held with his eyes.

The mere presence of Tyr and Thor
in the giants' home is a reminder of his failures

in an average life. They fall and break like so many of the half-realized goals one might set about to realize. Second place and participation trophies of life. But there is one piece of work which does not and that is the birthright of Tyr. Though he may not have what it takes to handle it himself, he is smart enough to be a part of tribe which will help him.

But the frith demanded of hospitality ensues and a fine meal is shared.

13. *Eight fell from the ledge,* | *and one alone,*

The hard-hammered kettle, | *of all was whole;*

Forth came they then, | *and his foes he sought,*

The giant old, | *and held with his eyes.*

14. *Much sorrow his heart* | *foretold when he saw*

The giantess' foeman | *come forth on the floor;*

Then of the steers | *did they bring in three;*

Their flesh to boil | *did the giant bid.*

It is interesting to note that Thor is known for killing more female than males of the race of giants. The masculine subdues the feminine. Each story has its own fine points. but for a giant, the representation of the grown but emotionally immature male, as in the case of Hymir it is a serious threat. Hymir is ruled by moods and lives with his mother and wife. There are a lot of heathens today in the same boat, big and strong enough to be considered men, but emotionally stunted and threatened at the loss of the feminine in their lives. The same can be said for women with the masculine in their lives. It is a frontier we can waste no more time on. The man and woman making ceremonies of our children will take on a newfound importance. These ceremonies should be done in the absence of the opposite sex and represent a complete severing of the ties. It is a key ingredient towards setting the table. Notice that this table barely had enough to satisfy the mighty hunger of Thor.

One might think that if this was the focus of the story, they would feast, and be done with it. But for some reason they decide to go on a fishin trip. The grizzled old giant and the mighty Thor head out to the water. A competition if you will for the moody braggart to display his prowess and prove to himself and himself alone that he might be capable of something worthwhile. Perhaps even on par with the Gods. Surely he could, had not his son endured a journey and been accepted as a member of this fine tribe which rules over everything it sees? He instructs Thor to secure his bait and balks at his suggestion to row even further out onto the ocean.

16. To the comrade hoary | of Hrungnir then

Did Hlorrithi's meal | full mighty seem;

"Next time at eve | we three must eat

The food we have | s the hunting's spoil."

17

Fain to row on the sea | was Veur, he said,

If the giant bold | would give him bait.

Hymir spake:

18. "Go to the herd, | if thou hast it in mind,

Thou slayer of giants, | thy bait to seek;

For there thou soon | mayst find, methinks,

Bait from the oxen | easy to get."

19. Swift to the wood | the hero went,

Till before him an ox | all black he found;

From the beast the slayer | of giants broke

The fortress high | of his double horns.

20. "Thy works, methinks, | are worse by far,

Thou steerer of ships, | than when still thou sittest."

21. The lord of the goats | bade the ape-begotten

Farther to steer | the steed of the rollers;

But the giant said | that his will, forsooth,

Longer to row | was little enough.

22. Two whales on his hook | did the mighty Hymir

Soon pull up | on a single cast;

In the stern the kinsman | of Othin sat,

And Veur with cunning | his cast prepared.

23. The warder of men, | the worm's destroyer,

Fixed on his hook | the head of the ox;

There gaped at the bait | the foe of the gods,

The girdler of all | the earth beneath.

24. The venomous serpent | swiftly up

To the boat did Thor, | the bold one, pull;

With his hammer the loathly | hill of the hair

Of the brother of Fenrir | he smote from above.

25. *The monsters roared, | and the rocks resounded,*

And all the earth | so old was shaken;

Then sank the fish | in the sea forthwith.

26.

Joyless as back | they rowed was the giant;

Speechless did Hymir | sit at the oars,

With the rudder he sought | a second wind.

In the midst of a simple fishing trip to secure food for a feast, Hymir is astonished and terrified that Thor raises the Midgard Serpent. Right here in front of him Thor has the chance to change the very tide of war and the outcome of Ragnarok. It must surely be a terrifying sight to find yourself in the presence of true greatness far beyond the well cultured ego of an online presence. Thor demonstrates that even in passing, his security as a powerful masculine symbol and God he has what it takes to change the world around him as he so pleases. When Thor is referred to as Veur, he is said to represent the vitality or life force of every man or woman. This is a terrifying thought to ponder for the being whose existence is still very much reactive to almost everything. The weather, the people we come across, the moods which dominate our thinking.

In some stories Hymir cuts the line. An example of the lengths to which the ego driven will go to prevent a change in the world which would demand a growing up if you will. An end of the ability to bluff ones' way through life by standing behind the false comfort of ceremony and self-importance. To cut the line of another mans' success before it overshadows your own is perhaps one of the great sins of existence and a denial of the true aspects of our being. In our world; these actions take the form of careful manipulations and half-hearted oaths from lesser men to prevent these ventures into the realm of development for the individual. Very rarely is something done to encourage this development. More often than not; half the story is told and then the insistence of an obligation or shyld because they didn't do the way we might have. Selfishness rules the roost and it does not foster the setting of a table where the gods might enjoin one to secure the finery one expects from a faith.

Twice more is Thor's strength tested and in the end, he has to slay the whole tribe.

Hymir spake:

~ 28 ~

27. "The half of our toil | wilt thou have with me,

And now make fast | our goat of the flood;

Or home wilt thou bear | the whales to the house,

Across the gorge | of the wooded glen?"

28. Hlorrithi stood | and the stem he gripped,

And the sea-horse with water | awash he lifted;

Oars and bailer | and all he bore

With the surf-swine home | to the giant's house.

29. His might the giant | again would match,

For stubborn he was, | with the strength of Thor;

None truly strong, | though stoutly he rowed,

Would he call save one | who could break the cup.

30. Hlorrithi then, | when the cup he held,

Struck with the glass | the pillars of stone;

As he sat the posts | in pieces he shattered,

Yet the glass to Hymir whole they brought.

31. But the loved one fair | of the giant found

A counsel true, | and told her thought:

"Smite the skull of Hymir, | heavy with food,

For harder it is | than ever was glass."

32. The goats' mighty ruler | then rose on his knee,

And with all the strength | of a god he struck;

Whole was the fellow's | helmet-stem,

But shattered the wine-cup | rounded was.

Hymir spake:

33. "Fair is the treasure | that from me is gone,

Since now the cup | on my knees lies shattered;"

So spake the giant: | "No more can I say

In days to be, | 'Thou art brewed, mine ale.'

34. "Enough shall it be | if out ye can bring

Forth from our house | the kettle here."

Tyr then twice | to move it tried,

But before him the kettle | twice stood fast.

35. The father of Mothi | the rim seized firm,

And before it stood | on the floor below;

Up on his head | Sif's husband raised it,

And about his heels | the handles clattered.

36. Not long had they fared, | ere backwards looked

The son of Othin, | once more to see;

From their caves in the east | beheld he coming

With Hymir the throng | of the many-headed.

37. He stood and cast | from his back the kettle,

And Mjollnir, the lover | of murder, he wielded;

So all the whales | of the waste he slew.

Twice it is mentioned that Thor is Sif's husband and mate all the while he is helping a member of his tribe secure something which is heritage but will benefit everyone. This is the kind of effort we need more of. Men and women who are willing to go the distance to help other members of the tribe heave to the waste which hampers their development. Men who are secure in their relationships and strong of mind and back. It is the confidence we are meant to breed in our own lives. And we can do it by following this example.

You see when we are in possession of a frame of mind that encourages a free give and take which is not laden with misbegotten ideals of selfishness, we are setting the table which will be a delight for the gods to enjoy. A frame of mind which is free from the petty nonsense we see so much of today and much of it was learned from men and women who knew; just absolutely knew, that when the time came they would be forgiven. No matter the damage they had done and the faulty thinking which they had engendered upon their greatest treasure. The going forth of a champion to secure the future of his tribe, his people and his organization is one of the greatest obligations we may ever undertake. It must be done with a frame of mind which is inviting to those high minded ideals of love so many of us are loathe to embrace. Therein lies the challenge of our greatness. Ask any soldier who has won a medal for heroism. Ask any mother who has risked everything for the safety of her children. Everything else was merely an after thought subsequent to the protection and safeguarding of those they loved and the feelings they helped create within them.

In all of this, we have taken a step towards securing the vessel necessary to brew a mead worthy of the gods. That unique substance which offers inspiration to so many of us and provides some small connection to the great stories of our past. If we have faced the fears such as Tyr has and secured a powerful positive friendship based on the goodwill of all; we have taken a powerful first step towards identifying the vessel we may need to brew the dreams and desires of our life. This will give us the ability to share them with everyone held close to us. Not to obligate them to us, but to encourage them that it can be done.

When it comes time to meet the steely eyed gaze of the one who would expect the most from us, have we relinquished the immature passions of a selfish child? It can be a powerful disappointment to look up and realize that after all this time walking the face of the earth that we might have missed the greatest challenge of our existence.

> *40. The mighty one came | to the council of gods,*
>
> *And the kettle he had | that Hymir's was;*
>
> *So gladly their ale | the gods could drink*
>
> *In Ægir's hall | at the autumn-time.*

To feast and drink in the autumn, during the harvest, speaks volumes of what we might expect if we grab on to these simple concepts and put them to us in our life. We are on every level simple aspects of the universe given form. From the atoms of carbon, iron, calcium and everything else which were born in the heart of stars to the divine gift of inspiration we are very much an integral part of the world around us.

We have what it takes to harness that, imbue it with divine power and put it to use for the betterment of not only our self, but everyone around us.

Now let's take a look at the table and its guests.

Chapter Two

There are times in our life when we may feel the constant pressure of not being good enough. The idea that all is lost or that you might not be able to accomplish it is a poisonous mental side note which has the ability to ruin any good meal. Our example is a well known story. It is one I have used in the past to outline the existence of evil in several contexts. But let's take a look at it with a different frame of mind. That we are well underway in our efforts to set a table for a divine feast within our own thinking process. Different, but no less valid.

One of the comments which inspired this train of thought was a comment I heard from a recording of Napolean Hill. He stated about a friend of his "Why, I don't believe the man would tolerate a negative thought!". This comment has always carried a lot of weight with me. The power of such mans' mental faculties must be astounding. Couple that with the fact that, at that time, he was worth roughly $600 million in the 1950's and it begins to lend credence to this notion of our thoughts become things. I've simply taken the example provided in our lore and fleshed out an idea to empower us. The example of setting a dinner party for those fine characteristics which our gods and goddesses represent to us. But the very instant we allow a negative thought to enter our minds, things can and will go sideways.

Ægir, who was also called Gymir, had prepared ale for the gods, after he had got the mighty kettle, as now has been told. To this feast came Othin and Frigg, his wife. Thor came not, as he was on a journey in the East. Sif, Thor's wife, was there, and Brag, with Ithun, his wife. Tyr, who had but one hand, was there; the wolf Fenrir had bitten off his other hand when they had bound him. There were Njorth and Skathi his wife, Freyr and Freyja, and Vithar, the son of Othin. Loki was there, and Freyr's servants Byggvir and Beyla. Many were there of the gods and elves.

The good and the greatest are assembled, just as we would like to be able to do with our own thoughts. To focus on the positive concepts the mention of these names brings to mind. To do so in a constant manner might bring about fantastic change to our lives. But just as Tyr and Thor had to struggle great in more than one aspect of their being, we will have to do some ground work to create a mindset where such ideas might flourish in our lives. But take careful note that in this warm-hearted feeling; we have left our great defender out of the loop. That focus is somewhere else, on some enemy far away and oblivious to the dangers within our own thinking.

Ægir had two serving-men, Fimafeng and Eldir. Glittering gold they had in place of firelight; the ale came in of itself; and great was the peace. The guests praised much the ability of Ægir's serving-men. Loki might not endure that, and he slew Fimafeng. Then the gods shook their shields and howled at Loki and drove him away to the forest, and thereafter set to drinking again. Loki turned back, and outside he met Eldir.

And there it is. All of the effort required of two Gods to support and encourage the development of the others to enjoy the company of heroes is destroyed in a minute. For just one thought, one being, one dinner guest who is possessed of selfishness to the extent that he cannot abide anyone achieving that which he cannot do on his own or be given, will ruin all our efforts. From there we must again take action to rid ourselves of these ruinous thoughts.

Usually a simple re-centering of ourselves and our goals is sufficient. The smile of our children, the encouraging word of our loved ones is usually all it takes to remind of how grateful we should be. But we are human and occasionally we will take a memory, a feeling or some failing of our past and re-examine it. We will revel in all the feeling until we tire of it and put it away. Sometimes though; we find ourselves in a challenging situation and we might find we are unable to do rid ourselves of this depressive state of being. If you will take a look around, you will see dozens, if not hundreds of individuals who thrive on the sympathy given to them because of any number of conditions. This kind of feedback loop is a difficult one to break. There is a legitimate fear in this persons eye that if they are no longer nourishing this or that pain; that people will not value them anymore. What will become of them? It becomes their identity. The work required to break down those walls can only originate from behind them. But I digress. Let's get back to that one negative thought/dinner guest. Such a thought may take a stroll through the carefully crafted mindset we have achieved and ridicule every single aspect of it.

Loki spoke to him:

1. "Speak now, Eldir, | for not one step

Farther shalt thou fare;

What ale-talk here | do they have within,

The sons of the glorious gods?"

Eldir spake:

2. *"Of their weapons they talk, | and their might in war,*

The sons of the glorious gods;

From the gods and elves | who are gathered here

No friend in words shalt thou find."

Loki spake:

3. *"In shall I go | into Ægir's hall,*

For the feast I fain would see;

Bale and hatred | I bring to the gods,

And their mead with venom I mix."

We know full well what happens when we begin to thinking and drinking. Everyone does. Some people do not even require the drink to start this process. But it is no different than this. "I'm going to engage in thinking which is not good for me." We mix the venom into the mead by ourselves. Bad things we have done, people we have hurt, the accumulated efforts and failures which have let those we love down, come back to haunt us. Try as we might, once we have started down this path, it can be very hard to put an end to it. Which brings me back to the idea that there once existed a man who would not tolerate a negative thought. That means I/we can do it too.

Eldir spake:

4. "If in thou goest | to Ægir's hall,

And fain the feast wouldst see,

And with slander and spite | wouldst sprinkle the gods,

Think well lest they wipe it on thee."

Loki spake:

5. "Bethink thee, Eldir, | if thou and I

Shall strive with spiteful speech;

Richer I grow | in ready words

If thou speakest too much to me."

The depressive state of mind is the antithesis of anything successful we might achieve. Even though we are well aware of it, once it has started there will be times for some people that there is very little one might say or do which would not be turned into some kind of self-loathing or personal hatred. All of those positive personal apsects of the divine which reside within us; at our request no less; are astounded when we allow even an inkling of these thoughts to gain traction. You see; it is our mind, we own it, and we control the thoughts which abound within it. We invite all of this positive force to help us along our way and then we introduce the past. If our focus has up til now been on the negative side, that's what we are going to find. It is an action which we have conditioned ourselves to perform. How many times have we thought to ourselves "this is too good to be true" and then watch the opportunity dry up or change in some unexpected way. When we perform the hard work of creating the perfect mindset to entertain the winners; it does not mean it is just a once and done kind of deal. It is a constant pleasant endeavor which has its' own rewards. If we; in the middle of this thinking process, introduce some bad memory, doubt or anger, our guests stand defenseless against our own neurosis.

Then Loki went into the hall, but when they who were there saw who had entered, they were all silent.

Loki spake:

6. "Thirsty I come | into this thine hall,

I, Lopt, from a journey long,

To ask of the gods | that one should give

Fair mead for a drink to me.

7. *"Why sit ye silent, | swollen with pride,*

Ye gods, and no answer give?

At your feast a place | and a seat prepare me,

Or bid me forth to fare."

This is the challenge of the arrogant and egotistical. That false bravado which proclaims we are more than the assembled patronage of our good and positive thoughts.

Bragi spake:

8. *"A place and a seat | will the gods prepare*

No more in their midst for thee;

For the gods know well | what men they wish

To find at their mighty feasts."

The very first God to address this bad apple is the god of poetry. Sweet talking is to no avail and it is immediately insulted. Common sense is thrown out the window. All of the good deeds we may have done are now scrutinized. Has any of it paid off? Or are we ignorant of the currency in which we are dealing?

Loki spake:

9. *"Remember, Othin, | in olden days*

That we both our blood have mixed;

Then didst thou promise | no ale to pour,

Unless it were brought for us both."

Othin spake:

10. "Stand forth then, Vithar, | and let the wolf's father

Find a seat at our feast;

Lest evil should Loki | speak aloud

Here within Ægir's hall."

Then Vithar arose and poured drink for Loki; but before he drank he spoke to the gods:

11. "Hail to you, gods! | ye goddesses, hail!

Hail to the holy throng!

Save for the god | who yonder sits,

Bragi there on the bench."

Bragi spake:

12. "A horse and a sword | from my hoard will I give,

And a ring gives Bragi to boot,

That hatred thou makst not | among the gods;

So rouse not the great ones to wrath."

Loki spake:

13. *"In horses and rings | thou shalt never be rich,*

Bragi, but both shalt thou lack;

Of the gods and elves | here together met

Least brave in battle art thou,

(And shyest thou art of the shot.)"

Bragi spake:

14. *"Now were I without | as I am within,*

And here in Ægir's hall,

Thine head would I bear | in mine hands away,

And pay thee the price of thy lies."

Loki spake:

15. *"In thy seat art thou bold, | not so are thy deeds,*

Bragi, adorner of benches!

Go out and fight | if angered thou feelest,

No hero such forethought has."

This kind of behavior, this abuse of the hospitality, is reminiscent of the online comments of men who have nothing to lose. Within it is the seed of ridiculousness, as much like the feasting hall where Loki knows he has nothing to lose, the internet hero; with his bold comments, also has nothing to lose. And just like that, our ability to keep a positive mindset is sucked in to a digital vortex which has absolutely nothing to do with our development in any manner whatsoever. Regaining our train of thought to focus on the positive becomes mired in "what are they saying about me?" and a host of other irrelevant thoughts. It is usually lesser men with something to prove who engage in such tripe. There is no effort required to back up the comments yet the digital age has allowed us the positive reinforcement of people who might take sides without any recrimination or challenge to their being. There is no struggle involved in it and it is a waste of time which erodes and eats away an enormous amount of resources within our minds which are better put to use in other arenas of our lives. The god of poetry is mistaken as weak, yet it is his words which write history and develop the narratives which guide us all. When we allow this type of negative thought into our thinking, we immediately cripple our ability to think highly of ourselves. There is no outside action anyone may take which has the ability to reduce, minimize or mitigate the divine presence within our self. It is only our own thoughts which do that.

Ithun spake:

16. "Well, prithee, Bragi, | his kinship weigh,

Since chosen as wish-son he was;

And speak not to Loki | such words of spite

Here within Ægir's hall."

Loki spake:

17. "Be silent, Ithun! | thou art, I say,

Of women most lustful in love,

Since thou thy washed-bright | arms didst wind

About thy brother's slayer."

Ithun spake:

18. "To Loki I speak not | with spiteful words

Here within Ægir's hall;

And Bragi I calm, | who is hot with beer,

For I wish not that fierce they should fight."

Next to go is youthful vigor. Our age becomes an issue. It doesn't matter if you are in college thinking about something in high school, or in your forties still fretting about some incident in your twenties. If only we were young again is truly a matter of degrees. If only we were possessed of the youthful vigor we had as children. Simple thoughts such as this have an almost immediate effect of severing the hamstring of ambition or motivation. We have allowed the negative to remove from our thoughts the ability to think of our self in a positive light and then we feel it. Those past youthful indiscretions or the people we may have hurt become again an item of thought. Even though there is every likelihood that you are the farthest thing from their mind. You are exactly where you need to be, no matter your age. The challenges in front of you are easily conquered. There are a plethora of examples of people who have achieved truly fantastic things in their later years. Great works of art, poetry, science abound from the wise elders of the human species. The only thing which is stopping you is you.

Gefjun spake:

19. "Why, ye gods twain, | with bitter tongues

Raise hate among us here?

Loki is famed | for his mockery foul,

And the dwellers in heaven he hates."

20. *"Be silent, Gefjun! | for now shall I say*

Who led thee to evil life;

The boy so fair | gave a necklace bright,

And about him thy leg was laid."

Othin spake:

21. *"Mad art thou, Loki, | and little of wit,*

The wrath of Gefjun to rouse;

For the fate that is set | for all she sees,

Even as I, methinks."

Gefjon is the divine feminine which leads the intro into the Prose Edda. She carved out a kingdom for herself and to an extent represents the very misunderstood feminine to the immature masculine. In an age when infant mortality was much higher, her position and reverence as a goddess who looked after the young girls who had passed on would have surely placed her in a positon of much importance. Be that as it may, in the feasting tradition the idea that a queen or princess might be fully aware of all of the goings on in a kingdom is important. On par with the Kings yet she says nothing. It is repeated in several chronicles of the past. Gefjon though; has been set loose upon Midgard and has an influence upon humanity which is almost on par with Rigs. In our minds though she is intuition. When we let loose that very negative energy and begin to be so focused on what is going wrong; we lose that very necessary gift of intuition. Intuition is that magical quality which allows us to trust our gut instinct and which women have and can use to miraculous effect. Right off the bat she can see that no good will come of this entire affair. If we have what it takes to be quiet, to silence the constant background noise of our thoughts, we might find we have that little voice as well. One that tells us we need not go down this path. That there is no need to entertain these types of guests, people in our lives and most especially these types of thoughts. Negativity robs us of that tool which acts as a compass towards the steps we need to take in order to achieve our goals.

Loki spake:

22. "Be silent, Othin! | not justly thou settest

The fate of the fight among men;

Oft gavst thou to him | who deserved not the gift,

To the baser, the battle's prize."

Othin spake:

23. "Though I gave to him | who deserved not the gift,

To the baser, the battle's prize;

Winters eight | wast thou under the earth,

Milking the cows as a maid,

(Ay, and babes didst thou bear;

Unmanly thy soul must seem.)"

Loki spake:

24. "They say that with spells | in Samsey once

Like witches with charms didst thou work;

And in witch's guise | among men didst thou go;

Unmanly thy soul must seem."

When Odin steps in to defend the use of intuition, a very important forerunner of wisdom, he is accused of unseemly acts too closely aligned with the feminine. He is defending one of his most important Asynjur. Odin understands what happens when we reject such a powerful aspect of our personality. Loki pays it no heed, much as we sometimes do and we will also lash out at those things we do not comprehend. Righteous indignation becomes our companion and hatred of any number of boogeymen appear. Races, creeds and colors appear to be aligned against us and we fail to focus on building our being. We instead shift gears to pointing the finger towards any perceived threat of that which we do not understand. Whether you wish to stand up for your convictions or sacrifice them for acceptance; the thinking process of those folk with this mindset will become immediately apparent to the wise. Think of this before you lash out.

There is also a ring of whining in this couple of stanzas which sounds like the petulant child "It's not fair! Why did/does he/she get this or that and not me?". We always know why someone else succeeds and we don't. It takes honesty but we will always know. They may have trained harder, they may have handled their money more responsibly, they may have made a commitment and kept to it. There are any number of actions a person may take to get ahead in this world and enjoy a very good life. If we let this type of dinner guest take a seat at the table of our feast we must be prepared to honestly deal with the very hard work of being honest with our self. At some point most people will have to do something of this nature. That is to clean house and take out the garbage of our thoughts. The question is; do you want to do it on your terms, or dive into it unprepared and half-cocked because we have thought ourselves into a corner and have no choice?

Frigg spake:

25. *"Of the deeds ye two | of old have done*

Ye should make no speech among men;

Whate'er ye have done | in days gone by,

Old tales should ne'er be told."

Loki spake:

26. *"Be silent, Frigg! | thou art Fjorgyn's wife,*

But ever lustful in love;

For Vili and Ve, | thou wife of Vithrir,

Both in thy bosom have lain."

Frigg spake:

27. *"If a son like Baldr | were by me now,*

Here within Ægir's hall,

From the sons of the gods | thou shouldst go not forth

Till thy fierceness in fight were tried."

Loki spake:

28. *"Thou wilt then, Frigg, | that further I tell*

Of the ill that now I know;

Mine is the blame | that Baldr no more

Thou seest ride home to the hall."

When the great mother speaks, people ought to pay attention. But to attack such a being which represents the nurturing spirit in which we were raised and in which we will be prepared for and escorted to the afterlife by; is to court disaster. True; some mothers are so only in the loosest sense of the word. But to focus upon that as the root source of the problems which are cascading through our thinking is a precarious path to tread. We are not qualified to cast any kind of blame against our mothers for the lovers they have had or the children they have lost. The confusion of the role the mother archetype plays within a persons' psyche is of such importance that the greatest minds of psychology have identified it as culprit in any number mental conditions. But there is one thing to remember; it will again remove our thoughts from that which they should be focused upon. On our being. No one else. Our actions are our own and to blame a mother for any failing is to seek to escape responsibility for life. To make peace with that and create a warm and inviting mindset where such a sense may prosper is to develop within our being the capacity to offer love for our children which they will always be grateful for. Just like any mother, Frigga does what she thinks is best for her children. To sacrifice that because of a mood is a mark of immaturity few people realize. You will see them yell from the rooftops when they are in this type of painful self-destruction. They will also wonder why they are alone.

Freyja spake:

29. *"Mad art thou, Loki, | that known thou makest*

The wrong and shame thou hast wrought;

The fate of all | does Frigg know well,

Though herself she says it not."

Loki spake:

30. *"Be silent, Freyja! | for fully I know thee,*

Sinless thou art not thyself;

Of the gods and elves | who are gathered here,

Each one as thy lover has lain."

Freyja spake:

31. *"False is thy tongue, | and soon shalt thou find*

That it sings thee an evil song;

The gods are wroth, | and the goddesses all,

And in grief shalt thou homeward go."

Loki spake:

32. "Be silent, Freyja! | thou foulest witch,

And steeped full sore in sin;

In the arms of thy brother | the bright gods caught thee

When Freyja her wind set free."

Our feast is now in shambles. We are so far deep into reminiscing about our various failures we have succumbed to the old feelings we thought we had dealt with when it comes to a broken heart. We dig deep into a bag of old hurts only to pull out a dusty old bauble covered in rust and assume it is still the treasure we once considered it. But it isn't, our sweat, tears and blood have rusted it to beyond recognition. Or; perhaps it is brand new and shiny. Anger has a tendency to overwhelm our thinking. There are any number of slights both real and imagined we might use against a person we were supposed to love so much at one time. We don't care who gets mad. In that finest instance of anger and resentment some of us are blessed with a truly profound decision with staggering implications.

Maybe we should try to reach out and give it another shot. For those few who actually do; the painful lesson of not even knowing what love is can be a most humiliating experience. It will leave an individual scratching their head wondering how it all went so wrong, what do I do now, how come it didn't get any better. The various lovers we have known now align to remind us of how much a fool we may have been. This type of drunken self-pity is most often associated with the lonely heart as they pine for love and find none. As they demand recognition and loudly declare themselves a suitable mate, yet alone they remain and wonder why. Doubt and uncertainty become our companions and the pain begins to morph into things which are dangerous and unnatural. For some folks this pain is the most prominent. Loneliness and blame coupled with self-pity can become the constant painful reminders of what could have been, or should have been, and there is always the thought of "if only".

In that frame of mind there is really only one thing you can do. Stop thinking. Take a good look around and take a quick positive mental inventory of this very moment. Not 10 minutes ago or a half hour from now. Not yesterday or tomorrow. But this very minute. It is all that we have. In this minute we need to realize as we are living and breathing we have a chance. It will give us the moment we need to realize we are ok and that the constant need for outside reinforcement is a misplaced effort. It is impossible to give something away we do not possess. Trying to allow someone you choose to love you until you can love yourself has led to more misery than people can begin to believe. Asatru turns that right around and reminds us that this must begin within our self. We have a chance to adopt principles of honesty with ourselves and others which would prevent us from continuing the cycle.

On the flip side of this particular coin we should always bear in mind that it is Freya who wears the Brisingammen Gem. These gems represent the fires of the human intellect and when we think about it we will become aware that the greatest works of architecture, poetry, music and the homes we live in are best brought to their highest point by that aspect of love. Love which feeds our brains a constant source of chemicals that make us feel good and see the world through new eyes. We should also remember that for all intents and purposes Freya is a single mother and yet she excels at being the Goddess she is. You have what it takes to step out of this as well. All by yourself, with or without the aid of others and it starts by loving who you are. Each positive action moving forward fills the well of our life with clean pure water. Over time it will dilute any drops of poison or bad blood which may have been dripped into the well. There is nothing more you can do to fix this contamination except be the best you possible moving forward. Don't waste another second of your life on a painful memory.

Njorth spake:

33. "Small ill does it work | though a woman may have

A lord or a lover or both;

But a wonder it is | that this womanish god

Comes hither, though babes he has borne."

Loki spake:

34. "Be silent, Njorth; | thou wast eastward sent,

To the gods as a hostage given;

And the daughters of Hymir | their privy had

When use did they make of thy mouth."

Njorth spake:

35. "Great was my gain, | though long was I gone,

To the gods as a hostage given;

The son did I have | whom no man hates,

And foremost of gods is found."

Loki spake:

36. "Give heed now, Njorth, | nor boast too high,

No longer I hold it hid;

With thy sister hadst thou | so fair a son,

Thus hadst thou no worse a hope."

When a person in the midst of such ego driven victim mentality is presented with an argument from a man who has everything; especially when it is evidenced by fantastic children, it will provide fodder for a good resentment and perhaps a day or two of just downright bitching. This is when the goodwill towards men, frith, grith and everything else flies out the window. I have heard many a grown man complaining about just such things. This is when we lash out with character assassination, usually with no other reason than this person is doing better than me. I have heard both men and women do it. Giving a loud voice to proclaiming their efforts only to have it swept away because someone else didn't like it. It becomes personal. When you get right down to it. No one cares. Life is going to go on and instead of whining for opportunity this is when we buckle down and begin to do our best. Once we have truly developed the best way to focus upon the work at hand to the best of our ability; this is when success begins to accompany our efforts. That success will also begin to change our mind. It will have an effect on our thinking process to see right action and hard work earn a just reward. Once we stop complaining about others, especially on the internet and focus our efforts on doing right and letting those actions speak for themselves we may well be at a turning point. This is where; for so many people; hope is again introduced into the thinking process and it becomes clearer.

Tyr spake:

37. "Of the heroes brave | is Freyr the best

Here in the home of the gods;

He harms not maids | nor the wives of men,

And the bound from their fetters he frees."

Loki spake:

38. "Be silent, Tyr! | for between two men

Friendship thou ne'er couldst fashion;

Fain would I tell | how Fenrir once

Thy right hand rent from thee."

Tyr spake:

39. *"My hand do I lack, | but Hrothvitnir thou,*

And the loss brings longing to both;

Ill fares the wolf | who shall ever await

In fetters the fall of the gods."

Loki spake:

40. *"Be silent, Tyr! | for a son with me*

Thy wife once chanced to win;

Not a penny, methinks, | wast thou paid for the wrong,

Nor wast righted an inch, poor wretch."

It will avail no one to brag about screwing someone else over. Especially a right and honorable man. Taking advantage of the good nature of people is nothing to be proud of. It is also something which will weigh on our thinking process in ways we cannot comprehend. Rights must be made to those we have harmed. There is a special place in the halls of Hel's realm for men who seduce the wives of other men. This is just not a place any man should ever venture. If we are having a difficult time with the normal problems society throws upon us as soon as we walk out of the door, what do you think will happen when we exacerbate the problem with a situation for which there is no easy solution? It is warned against in the Havamal in a couple of places. For us it is a trap. It is a problem which will ensure the cancerous leech of egoic thinking will help us to remain in this thinking process for a long, long time. Bitter and old, with a heart festering with the puss of guilt is not how I intend to grow old.

Freyr spake:

41. "By the mouth of the river | the wolf remains

Till the gods to destruction go;

Thou too shalt soon, | if thy tongue is not stilled,

Be fettered, thou forger of ill."

Loki spake:

42. "The daughter of Gymir | with gold didst thou buy,

And sold thy sword to boot;

But when Muspell's sons | through Myrkwood ride,

Thou shalt weaponless wait, poor wretch."

Here we have a god who provides us with a glance at the courage necessary to love properly. No matter the cost, he will give his heart to another and never shy away from the consequences. Imagine if we set a place at the table for such a being in our thinking process. To find courage and a resolute desire to love with all of our heart. Knowing full well when the time comes, the greatest fire around will burn him to the ground. Though fight he will. And now it is our turn to fight. Stand up, shake all of these notions of self-pity and failure off of our shoulders and take that first brave step forward into a future you desire. Frey is the everyman and his courage in the face of destiny does not hamper him from achieving that to which he has set his heart. His life will be full and pleasant. Yours will as well.

Byggvir spake:

43. "Had I birth so famous | as Ingunar-Freyr,

And sat in so lofty a seat,

I would crush to marrow | this croaker of ill,

And beat all his body to bits."

Loki spake:

44. "What little creature | goes crawling there,

Snuffling and snapping about?

At Freyr's ears ever | wilt thou be found,

Or muttering hard at the mill."

Byggvir spake:

45. "Byggvir my name, | and nimble am I,

As gods and men do grant;

And here am I proud | that the children of Hropt

Together all drink ale."

Loki spake:

46. "Be silent, Byggvir! | thou never couldst set

Their shares of the meat for men;

Hid in straw on the floor, | they found thee not

When heroes were fain to fight."

The serving man speaks out against the one who threatens the hope Frey offers to men. To dare to enjoy life. In our minds, this serving man should be a sound voice calling us back to reason and encouraging us to set a table for a feast of life we will enjoy. This may also be considered one of our friends who sees what we are worth.

Heimdall spake:

47. *"Drunk art thou, Loki, | and mad are thy deeds,*

Why, Loki, leavst thou this not?

For drink beyond measure | will lead all men

No thought of their tongues to take."

Loki spake:

48. *"Be silent, Heimdall! | in days long since*

Was an evil fate for thee fixed;

With back held stiff | must thou ever stand,

As warder of heaven to watch."

The whitest of the Asa and the guardian of the bridge is a sentinel for what may come and go in our own minds. It is Heimdall who slays Loki in the end of all things. But for us, he is a protector for the feast we may be beginning to see. A feast of life we want for our self. Now we have come across the guardian and he clearly points out what it is which helps enable this poisonous thinking. Too much drink. Heimdall is a light in the darkness and a defender of this feast we are going to setting. A light to shine upon our thinking and keep it positive.

Skathi spake:

49. *"Light art thou, Loki, | but longer thou mayst not*

In freedom flourish thy tail;

On the rocks the gods bind thee | with bowels torn

Forth from thy frost-cold son."

Loki spake:

50. "Though on rocks the gods bind me | with bowels
torn

Forth from my frost-cold son,

I was first and last | at the deadly fight

There where Thjazi we caught."

Skathi spake:

51. "Wert thou first and last | at the deadly fight

There where Thjazi was caught,

From my dwellings and fields | shall ever come forth

A counsel cold for thee."

Loki spake:

52. "More lightly thou spakest | with Laufey's son,

When thou badst me come to thy bed;

Such things must be known | if now we two

Shall seek our sins to tell."

And finally we come face to face with something we may have done which compromises a true injury to the community around us. How do we deal with that? What are we capable of doing which will allow us to rid the mind of a constant reminder of failure? I have and do know men who have committed such acts which are far beyond the comprehension of people dealing with everyday life. Soldiers and convicts both. I can tell you one thing. That we must overcome the conditioning we have heretofore subscribed to as being important in our lives and seek out a new path with the seriousness of life and death. Servicemen, public servants, convicts are at especially high risk for this particular breed of depressing thought. Given the chance, this weed finds fertile ground to grow in to a most troublesome pest in our garden of thoughts. The thing is, just like with this feast, it only blossoms under certain conditions. When just one negative thought or aspect appears in our thinking process, it is all too easy for it to cascade uncontrollably into something much worse than it is. We must remain vigilant in keeping our thoughts focused in such a manner that it would invite the divine to join us. Perhaps we might rely upon Heimdall to guard our thoughts. Maybe it is the reason he makes his appearance before this exchange between Loki and Skadi. Whatever the case; it reminds us to keep our thoughts positive. Given an inch, negative thoughts will take a mile

Then Sif came forward and poured mead for Loki in a crystal cup, and said:

53. "Hail too thee, Loki, | and take thou here

The crystal cup of old mead;

For me at least, | alone of the gods,

Blameless thou knowest to be."

He took the horn, and drank therefrom:

54. "Alone thou wert | if truly thou wouldst

All men so shyly shun;

But one do I know | full well, methinks,

Who had thee from Hlorrithi's arms,--

(Loki the crafty in lies.)"

How often has a spouse attempted to help us only to have it thrown back in their face. All the while accepting the crystal cup of mead. One of the greatest challenges is to be kind to those closest to us when we are feeling this way. In all of these interchanges; each god or goddess steps up to defend the next one. And in our thinking each corrosive, negative thought eats away at a positive one. It can create a very difficult atmosphere for those we love. But we should not create a back door for our self to engage in this type of detrimental thinking by abusing the ones we love. That kind of guilt is just another way our ego will trick us into the same old story time after time. Be aware of it. Try to remember that these people are around us because they want to be. We should not make them regret that decision.

Real trouble begins when both parties involved are feeding off of the same mental process by which the various failures are the fault of the partner. These people will either figure it out or continue a downward spiral with a built excuse. Entire volumes have been written concerning such relationships and a true expose on the difficulties and depth of neurosis involved is far outside the scope of this book. Suffice it to say, someone will eventually need to change in one way or another. This is not always a positive change. Most of the time it is a sacrifice of various aspects of a partner. This is done to avoid dealing with the difficulties involved in the other partners' actions and words. This is not what a healthy relationship is and there is always someone else who will consider you worth much more. But it must start with you. You've got to value yourself first.

With regards to our children, I always try to remember that I am all that they have and live up to that idea. It is in the action of loving our partners and children that we will find release from the background noise burdening our minds.

Beyla spake:

55. "The mountains shake, | and surely I think

From his home comes Hlorrithi now;

He will silence the man | who is slandering here

Together both gods and men."

Loki spake:

56. "Be silent, Beyla! | thou art Byggvir's wife,

And deep art thou steeped in sin;

A greater shame | to the gods came ne'er,

Befouled thou art with thy filth."

Again a servant comes forth to remind us to stop all of this negativity. Another friend if you will. These gods and goddesses, these aspects of our personal power and divinity are here to assist us in life. The next step is where we go to war with our self.

Then came Thor forth, and spake:

57. "Unmanly one, cease, | or the mighty hammer,

Mjollnir, shall close thy mouth;

Thy shoulder-cliff | shall I cleave from thy neck,

And so shall thy life be lost."

Loki spake:

58. "Lo, in has come | the son of Earth:

Why threaten so loudly, Thor?

Less fierce thou shalt go | to fight with the wolf

When he swallows Sigfather up."

Thor spake:

59. "Unmanly one, cease, | or the mighty hammer,

Mjollnir, shall close thy mouth;

I shall hurl thee up | and out in the East,

Where men shall see thee no more."

Loki spake:

60. "That thou hast fared | on the East-road forth

To men shouldst thou say no more;

In the thumb of a glove | didst thou hide, thou great one,

And there forgot thou wast Thor."

Thor spake:

61. "Unmanly one, cease, | or the mighty hammer,

Mjollnir, shall close thy mouth;

My right hand shall smite thee | with Hrungnir's slayer,

Till all thy bones are broken."

Loki spake:

62. "Along time still | do I think to live,

Though thou threatenest thus with thy hammer;

Rough seemed the straps | of Skrymir's wallet,

When thy meat thou mightest not get,

(And faint from hunger didst feel.)"

Thor spake:

63. "Unmanly one, cease, | or the mighty hammer,

Mjollnir, shall close thy mouth;

The slayer of Hrungnir | shall send thee to hell,

And down to the gate of death."

Loki spake:

64. *"'I have said to the gods | and the sons of the god,*

The things that whetted my thoughts;

But before thee alone | do I now go forth,

For thou fightest well, I ween.

65. *"Ale hast thou brewed, | but, Ægir, now*

Such feasts shalt thou make no more;

O'er all that thou hast | which is here within

Shall play the flickering flames,

(And thy back shall be burnt with fire.)"

The argument between Loki and Thor is reminiscent of the tug of war which may rage in our thoughts. It has been portrayed in various forms of media as the devil on one shoulder and the angel on another. The comedic effect is to go with the devil. But the real life need is to defend our thoughts from those ideas we might consider important but are in reality a corrosive thread throughout everything we have built. Thor is the warder and protector of men. He is readily available and well respected in both old and new times. Whenever the ego is faced with such a powerful aspect of personal confidence its pitiful arguments are ineffectual and ridiculous. When a failure is pointed out to the confident man or woman, the remembrance is of one where they got up to try it again. Thor does not engage in any idle talk, he sticks to one point and repeats it three times. When a person who has struggled with all of the different arguments we have just discussed is in the middle of it, we should adopt the same mentality as Thor does. We stick to the one positive point we know and we repeat it to ourselves until such time as the challenge passes. Bolstered with the strength of a god, such negativity flees in the face of a powerful confidence and one who now has control of his own mind. We have what it takes to get up and try it again else we wouldn't have made it this far. Now go through and begin to bind up these thoughts in a similar manner as the gods have with the corruptor of the feast. Loki has no true idea of how the divine interacts with each other. Neither do the thoughts in your head, which seek to drag you down and drown you in your own negativity, understand how the thinking of positive thoughts are going to change the world around you. But they will. And before you know it there will come a time when these great struggles cease to be any kind of issue in your life.

And after that Loki hid himself in Franang's waterfall in the guise of a salmon, and there the gods took him. He was bound with the bowels of his son Vali, but his son Narfi was changed to a wolf. Skathi took a poison-snake and fastened it up over Loki's face, and the poison dropped thereon. Sigyn, Loki's wife, sat there and held a shell under the poison, but when the shell was full she bore away the poison, and meanwhile the poison dropped on Loki. Then he struggled so hard that the whole earth shook therewith; and now that is called an earthquake.

It can be tough to read these concepts which I have put forth. In each case even I have been tempted to think "well I would never do that" or "I didn't really act that badly", in heathenry there is a worse excuse "I'm a heathen and I don't apologize for anything." But in adopting that mentality, there is an obligation not to act in such a manner to begin with. It is a struggle we must adopt.

Each one of us has a unique perspective on any of these ideas I have put forth, but none of us have created a new emotion. If you wish to escape those gray days and black nights I urge you to find yourself within these words and dedicate your mind to building a feasting hall, replete with its own brewing vessel in which to brew the great ideas of your life. It is your mind. The thoughts which fill it are your choice and your choice alone. Invite the gods to feast in the halls of your mind and fill it with the type of positive mindset one always sees with the well to do and successful.

Chapter Three

We have the option to entertain greatness. We have the gifts necessary to conquer what challenges are in front of us. This is by no means an attempt to deny the seriousness of the truly painful events people will face in their life. But it is an attempt to encourage people to focus their thoughts on what truly matters. The pain will subside, if we let it. If we allow one such as what Loki represents repeatedly enter the great hall of our thoughts and our minds we will continue to live much as his daughter Hel. Her hall is a much less favorable affair.

Hel he cast into Niflheim, and gave to her power over nine worlds, to apportion all abodes among those that were sent to her: that is men dead of sickness or of old age. Sha has great possessions there; her walls are exceeding high and her gates are great. Her hall is called Sleet-cold; her dish, Hunger; Famine is her knife; idler, her thrall; Sloven, her maidservant; Pit of Stumbling, her threshold, by which one enters; Disease her bed; Gleaming Bale, her bed hangings.

For those of us who have endured depression, anxiety, fear, loneliness, abandonment, drug addiction, drunkenness and a host of other feelings or conditions, these surroundings appear as familiar as our favorite pair of jeans or shoes. We wear them again and again. They are not waiting for us in an afterlife of some kind, we are dealing with them right now. By binding those negative thoughts as they appear, keeping our chin up and the constant repetition of the ideal setting you would wish to create for the gods to be entertained, we can secure a new foothold on life. One which we may have expected when we began this journey in Asatru. Asatru offers a choice and lays out a simple idea along spiritual lines we might adopt. It is my sincere desire that this book might be able to assist those folk who still suffer from these conditions. Even if it is no more than an understanding that maybe it is time to seek help.

All through our lives we will be given glimpses of hope. Most of the time people have been conditioned to immediately reject these notions. We are taught that everything good must come from outside of our self, that someone will come along to help us. The white knight rescuing the damsel in distress, the good woman who finds the love of a diamond in the rough. It's a dream which has been foisted upon us from the beginning. The confusion of its abject failure is evident throughout almost every level of society. It may well be the impetus for this rebirth of hope for the individual. People are beginning to understand that we are going to have to take the reigns and handle our own lives.

Once that idea firmly took root in my mind and then I discovered that my thoughts were my own. I found a freedom from the pinball effect of life which drives so many people absolutely razy. It also freed me from the need to continue dealing with people who are not worth my time. Why should you?

We each have something we would wish to accomplish, some goal or idea we expect for our lives. If there is someone in your life whose sole purpose is to manipulate, coerce, or just be a wet blanket on every idea you come up with, you might need to figure out how to deal with them at arms-length. I say arms-length because you need to see if there is any truth to what they are saying. Do they have a point? More importantly have you been determining the worth of your being based upon their opinion. Less safe by far is the wisdom found in another mans' heart.

The majority of people are going to be looking out for their own best interests, and they should, no one else is going to do it. It is in our best interests to determine if their interests and ours are congruent. If so; then work together, build success for each other. But when it is no longer feasible, we should never feel guilt or shame for standing up for ourselves and having the courage to say "no". Their opinion of you will not in any way change the amount of divine energy within you. Your ability to say "no" is what will prevent the opening of a door which allows in resentment, anger, frustrations and any of a host of negative thoughts which will all change the dynamic of your thinking. Just as the inability to do so did with Aegir's feast. The negative idea/aspect was told to leave once over a terrible transgression against the frith of the gathering. And just like our own thinking or affairs with other people, we are tempted to think, "well, it'll be different this time!". Unless we have dramatically changed who we are and how we think, the result will be the same. And that is the whole purpose of this book. To help us identify as many of those thoughts which have plagued us in the past and see them for what they are. Then; to get rid of them.

The view of what our future may look like is written:

59. Now do I see | the earth anew

Rise all green | from the waves again;

The cataracts fall, | and the eagle flies,

And fish he catches | beneath the cliffs.

60. *The gods in Ithavoll | meet together,*

Of the terrible girdler | of earth they talk,

And the mighty past | they call to mind,

And the ancient runes | of the Ruler of Gods.

61. *In wondrous beauty | once again*

Shall the golden tables | stand mid the grass,

Which the gods had owned | in the days of old,

62. *Then fields unsowed | bear ripened fruit,*

All ills grow better, | and Baldr comes back;

Baldr and Hoth dwell | in Hropt's battle-hall,

And the mighty gods: | would you know yet more?

63. *Then Honir wins | the prophetic wand,*

And the sons of the brothers | of Tveggi abide

In Vindheim now: | would you know yet more?

64. *More fair than the sun, | a hall I see,*

Roofed with gold, | on Gimle it stands;

There shall the righteous | rulers dwell,

And happiness ever | there shall they have.

The cultivation of the best aspect of our personalities and association with the divine is done so we might enjoy this outcome as well. Yep, you will most likely be an entirely different person. But isn't that what we want. That person we believed in when we were young and strong, beautiful and lithe, or even younger when we were kids and there was still magic in our world. There are a lot of people who use Asatru as an escape, imagine the surprise of the faithful when they discover there are tools here which can help us build something every bit as grand as we might have imagined. What have you got to lose?

Chapter Four

One of the best ways to enjoy the feedback of our successes is to handle the little details of our life. Let's say you have a particular area of your life from which you receive the majority of the positive feedback in your life. Perhaps it is work, or a hobby maybe it is sports or physical fitness. The dedication with which you pursue the goals you set for yourself and the subsequent positive feedback from that development is reflected to you in a certain manner. It is what we are expecting, we get it and we continue on. But there are many areas of a persons' life which create a well rounded individual.

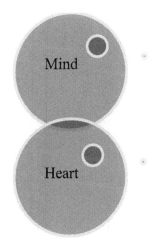

Family

Work

Hobbies

Spirituality

It may look something like the above image. Your mind and heart are aligned in such a manner that they might focus on the one thing which provides the most positive feedback. The biggest bang for the buck if you will. But what happens if your focus is somewhat out of balance with the regards to the rest of them. Let's say that the majority of your focus is on your hobby. A lot of people do this. It is something which we might truly enjoy. We will spend money and time on it. But we might neglect the other three areas of our life. Well; what does that really matter? You've done what I and many others like myself have suggested, you have focused on what you love. You will be receiving your positive reinforcement from just one area of your life.

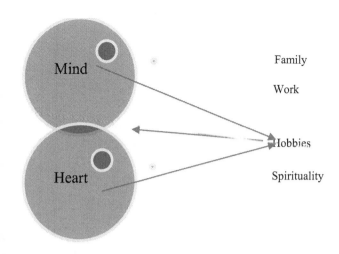

Mind

Heart

Family

Work

Hobbies

Spirituality

But the things which we neglect tend to weigh on our minds. When there is the constant background noise of the things we are not handling murmuring in our heads it has the same effect as placing a filter on the feedback we are expecting and in some cases craving. This is how those unbidden negative guests arrive at the feast we are attempting to create. So we might redouble our efforts and spend even more time and money on it. The sensation of not quite getting what we want may nag at us from the corner of our minds. It might look like this. People call it buyers remorse or obsessive and compulsive, or any number of modern labels, but all we are doing is seeking the best manner to enjoy this feedback.

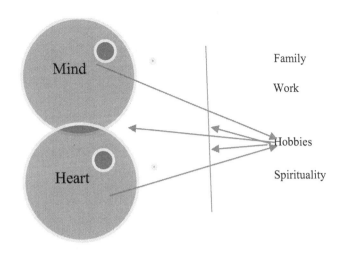

Mind

Heart

Family

Work

Hobbies

Spirituality

This is a natural mechanism at work in the human body. The pleasure center of the brain and the artificial stimulation of it has become an art. Just ask any person in marketing. Drugs, Gambling, Porn, all of these things and many more represent a very greedy aspect of our being which is way out of natural proportion. But in a world which is already very much out of balance; even figuring out that we are out of whack is a challenge. We are always going to do the thing which we enjoy the most, but what no one has told us, is that if we do not handle the rest of our existence with as much diligence as our hobby we are shortchanging our self.

If we can take those few minutes to put as much focus on the other areas of life we enjoy we will find that we will be receiving much more positive feedback than we planned. As we handle those seemingly small details of life we begin to remove that filter which is blocking the full enjoyment of our hobby. The nagging thoughts that "we need to do this" or "I forgot to do that" can be silenced if we will handle things as we are able. If we cannot do it right then, make the preparations to handle things as possible. But stop letting these things dominate the background noise of your thoughts and deny you the positive feedback you are more than capable of delivering to yourself. We are also enjoying the positive feedback associated with the other areas of our life. The payback is tenfold and it is a solid foundation for a good, good life.

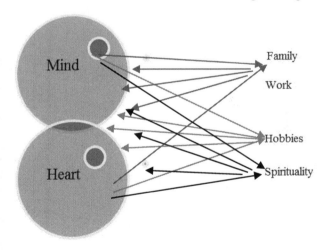

This is how we put the effort into life to enjoy it. Just like the grain of wheat, when the seed is planted it yields a harvest of much more than was put into the ground. These are just off the cuff examples and your life most likely contains many more areas of importance. But the principle is the same. We handle the details of life as they arise and we prevent the negative ideas which arise when we know we can do better. If you want to imagine that feedback as money or love, respect or fame, however you wish to picture it. If you will focus on what you love and understand that so much more of it may be enjoyed if we handle every area of our life with the same fortitude the biggest fear you will have to face is "What happens when it all comes true?" I say "Let's go find out!"

Made in the USA
Lexington, KY
13 September 2019